SHE'S STILL THERE

STUDY GUIDE

SHE'S STILL THERE

Rescuing the Girl in You

STUDY GUIDE
SIX SESSIONS

CHRYSTAL EVANS HURST

WITH KEVIN AND SHERRY HARNEY

ZONDERVAN

She's Still There Study Guide
Copyright © 2017 by Chrystal Evans Hurst

This title is also available as a Zondervan ebook.

Requests for information should be addressed to:
Zondervan, 3900 Sparks Dr., SE, Grand Rapids, MI 49546

ISBN 978-0-310-08173-9

Cover illustrations: AlienValley / Creative Market
Interior design: Kait Lamphere

First Printing June 2017 / Printed in the United States of America

CONTENTS

A WORD FROM
CHRYSTAL EVANS HURST

As a young girl, my parents encouraged me to live with wonder. My teachers gave me the courage to explore, my friends allowed me the chance to play, and my world offered me the opportunity to learn and grow. Fall and spring days were full with homework, school activities, and play with neighborhood friends. The summer months held visits to my grandparents, slumber parties with cousins, and long, boring days with an occasional trip to the library.

I had hopes and dreams and a picture of what my grown-up life might look like. I imagined my future family, my future career, and all the future places I would live. I figured I would either be a teacher or a famous actress and that I would live close to my family but have a second home near the beach. Every book I read and every person I met introduced me to more of the world that I could experience.

My youth wasn't perfect, but less-than-perfect didn't stop me from growing. I accepted my childhood for what it was: part of the process of my progress through life. I leaned into the living, believing that all the beautiful and unpleasant parts of my current and future picture would someday make sense if I just kept going. I believed all parts of my life—the good, the bad, and the ugly—could come together in the hands of the person who gave me life.

Fast-forward several years into the future. I am driving down the tollway in Dallas, headed home from another day at work, where I had spent hours stuffed in a cubicle, checking a million boxes with a red pen. My brain is about to explode. I hate my job.

The clock crawls from the moment I sit in my chair until the time it is reasonable for me to run out the door at the end of the day. It feels as if I am gasping for fresh air.

In that moment, I pray, *God, if you would just break both of my legs, that would make everything better.* In my stressed-out, overwhelmed, off-track mode of thinking, I wish for the shelter of a hospital room to provide some time to assess where I had gotten off track and formulate a plan for making my life more like I had imagined it would be.

I hadn't intended to end up in a job I didn't love. I hadn't intended to be a single parent. I hadn't intended to have a heart still raw from the hurt imposed by others. It had never been my dream to fight my way through the academic challenges and personal struggles of my college years only to end up feeling deflated. I had filled my balloon of hope with expectations and dreams only to realize that I had not tied it tightly enough.

I would love to tell you that in those moments driving down the tollway and thinking like a crazy person, I magically gained clarity on how I had gotten off track. I'd like to say that I never got off track again. I would love to tell you that I figured all of it out right then and there and that I've had it all figured out since.

The truth is that I haven't solved everything. I have gained an understanding over time, which is what I will share with you in this study, but I still don't have all the answers. But the truth is also that I *didn't* self-destruct that day in the car. I chose to keep driving. Even while the tears streamed down my face and I cried out to God for help. I kept going for one reason and one reason alone: *I believed my girl was still there.*

Even if she seemed lost, invisible, and forgotten, I believed that God could still make a masterpiece out of her. Maybe you've felt the same way. Maybe you've been a crazy woman like me and begged God to help you fix your life, get unstuck, and get it together. Maybe you've thought about what extreme measure you could take to stop the pain and heartache.

If so, I want to tell you that *your girl is still there.* Your uniquely beautiful life is an original work of art designed for your good and for the glory of the one who orchestrated your existence . . . even if it doesn't look like it at this moment. You are allowed to be both a masterpiece and a work in progress simultaneously. Your life matters. The girl of your dreams matters. No matter how far you think you've drifted away from her, *she's still there.*

My prayer is that at the end of this study, you will be motivated to get to the business of choosing to believe in the gift of "you." My hope is that you will act as if the girl in you is still there and be willing to do whatever it takes to participate in her rescue. Most important, I pray that you will choose to give the gift of understanding, encouragement, and truth to someone else who needs to believe her life still matters. We girls need each other.

Chrystal

HOW TO USE THIS GUIDE

The *She's Still There* video study is designed to be experienced in a group setting such as a Bible study, Sunday school class, or any small-group gathering. Each session begins with a brief opening reflection and "talk about it" questions to get you and your group thinking about the topic. You will then watch a video with Chrystal Evans Hurst and jump into some directed small-group discussion. You will close each session with a time of prayer as a group.

Each person in the group should have her own study guide, which includes video teaching notes, Bible study and group discussion questions, and between-sessions personal studies to help you reflect on and apply the material to your life during the week. You are also encouraged to have a copy of the *She's Still There* book, as reading the book alongside the curriculum will provide you with deeper insights and make the journey more meaningful. See the "recommended reading" section at the end of each session for the chapters in the book that correspond to material you and your group are discussing.

To get the most out of your group experience, keep the following points in mind. First, the real growth in this study will happen during your small-group time. This is where you will process the content of Chrystal's message, ask questions, and learn from others as you hear what God is doing in their lives. For this reason, it is important for you to be fully committed to the group and attend each session so you can build trust and rapport with the other members. If you choose to only "go through the motions," or if you refrain from participating, there is a lesser chance you will find what you're looking for during this study.

Second, remember that the goal of your small group is to serve as a place where people can share, learn about God, and build intimacy and friendship. For this reason, seek to make your group a "safe place." This means being honest about your thoughts and feelings and listening carefully to everyone else's opinion. (If you are a group leader, there are additional instructions and resources in the back of the book for leading a productive discussion group.)

Third, resist the temptation to "fix" a problem someone might be having or to correct her theology, as that's not the purpose of your small-group time. Also, keep everything your group shares confidential. This will foster a rewarding sense of community in your group and create a place where people can heal, be challenged, and grow spiritually.

Following your group time, maximize the impact of the course with the additional between-session studies. For each session, you may wish to complete the personal study all in one sitting or spread it out over a few days (for example, working on it a half-hour a day on four different days that week). Note that if you are unable to finish (or even start!) your between-sessions personal study, you should still attend the group study video session. You are still wanted and welcome at the group even if you don't have your "homework" done.

Keep in mind this study is an opportunity for you to train in a new way of seeing yourself and your walk with God. The videos, discussions, and activities are simply meant to kick-start your imagination so you are not only open to what God wants you to hear but also how to apply it to your life. As you go through this study, be watching for what God is saying as it relates to fighting for your life, looking at your life in a new way, embracing the life He has given you, developing your life according to His plan, finding encouragement in your life, and ultimately choosing the life that you want to lead.

OF NOTE: The introduction and quotations in this study guide are excerpted from the book *She's Still There* and the video curriculum of the same name. The other resources in the guide (including the session introductions, small-group questions, and between-sessions materials) were written by Kevin and Sherry Harney in collaboration with Chrystal Evans Hurst. Also, if you are a group leader, note that additional instructions and resources have been provided in the back of this guide to help you lead your group members through the study.

FIGHT FOR YOUR LIFE

You have to choose to be brave enough to believe that a uniquely beautiful life is still yours to have. And you have to choose to be bold enough to grab hold of the hope you have for the girl inside. The girl who's still there. The girl who dreamed of—and deserves—her beautiful life.

Chrystal Evans Hurst

Opening Reflection

Carmen started college with hope and excitement overflowing in her heart. She had grown up in a loving church family and had a solid footing in God's Word. Through high school her faith had been strong and real, and most of the students respected her for it. She felt confident as she continued her educational journey at a state university. But in a matter of weeks, her entire world changed. Her professors challenged her faith, her roommates had lifestyles that were dramatically different than her own, and no one seemed to respect her faith commitments the way they had back home. Early one Sunday morning, Carmen found herself walking a desolate and quiet campus as she went to a local church. She felt alone and feared a dark cloud of depression was beginning to settle on her life.

Margaret and Carlos were celebrating their ten-year anniversary in the delivery room. What a serendipitous surprise! It looked as if their third child would be born on the same day they had said, "I do!" They both knew what to expect. The pregnancy had gone without a hitch. But something took a shocking turn in the delivery room. The couple could see it on the doctor's face. They could feel it in the nurses' strained voices. When their son was finally delivered, they entered a season that would include two months of visiting him in the hospital every day, six more months of special care with nurses visiting their home, and a lifetime of challenges due to physical limitations they had never anticipated.

Theresa sat at the kitchen table looking out the window. This was the table where she, Ty, and their children had eaten countess meals, laughed until it hurt, argued about the little stuff of life, prayed, and become a family together. As she sat there, she could see the kids and Ty on the screen of her mind. Toddlers, children, teens... each scene a precious memory. Now the kids were all grown and gone. The table was empty...it was now just her. After forty-six years of marriage, with all of its highs and lows, Ty had gone home to be with Jesus. The funeral was over, the guests had gone, and the fridge was packed full of food and desserts brought by family, neighbors, and church members.

Every stage of life provides opportunities for inexpressible joy but also heart-numbing pain. Every person who walks on this planet discovers that the landmines of sorrow, loss, struggle, and heartache are plentiful—and it is never certain exactly where they are. The question is not *whether* we will experience pain on this earth. Rather, the question is, will we be committed to *fight* for our lives and hold on to Jesus when the hard times come?

Talk About It

Welcome to the first session of *She's Still There*. If you or any of your fellow group members do not know one another, take a few minutes to introduce yourselves. Next, to get things started, discuss one of the following questions:

- What is something you've asked God to do in a moment of frustration or doubt, and now, looking back, you are glad He didn't do it?

or

- What are some things that you are committed to fight for in this life and hold on to even in tough times?

Video Teaching Notes

Play the video segment for session one. As you watch, use the following outline to record any thoughts or concepts that stand out to you.

When you feel lost in life, you have to be willing to *fight* for change to occur. Are you willing to cooperate and participate with God in what He wants to do within you?

The Bible states *what* you are: *God's workmanship* or *masterpiece* (see Ephesians 2:10). You need to believe this truth about yourself even when you don't feel that it is true.

The disconnect often occurs because you are a *work in progress*. You are transforming into a masterpiece—and things can get messy in the middle of the process. The Bible is filled with stories of people who had "messy" times as they grew to become God's masterpieces.

The Bible says *how* you are God's masterpiece: because you have been created in Christ Jesus. You are God's masterpiece when you are physically born, and you are God's masterpiece when you are spiritually reborn in Christ.

The Bible says *why* you are God's masterpiece: you were created for good works. You are a physical creature who has a spiritual purpose. The temptation is to quit when you get into the messy middle, but you have to believe God has a finished work in mind for you.

The love of God that saves your soul will also change your life. As you receive God's love and participate with Him in the process of transformation, He takes you from where you are to where He wants you to be. You just accept His love and participate in the process.

If you are going to believe you are spiritually wealthy, it should affect your spiritual walk. If you believe how God sees you in Christ, it should change how the world sees Christ in you. It's not enough to just accept you are a masterpiece without taking action on it.

Feeling lost does not equal lifelessness. You have the ability to partner with God and change your life's course—to "fight the good fight of the faith" (1 Timothy 6:12).

Bible Study and Group Discussion

Take a few minutes with your group members to discuss what you just watched and explore these concepts in Scripture.

1. There's a difference between just living life and really living the best life that God has intended for us. What does it look like when we are just "living life"? How can this change when we start to experience the fullness of the life God has for us?

2. Think about a time you entered a situation that looked good and positive but ended up being difficult and painful. How did that season impact your spiritual life, particularly your prayers?

    Think about a time you found yourself crying out to God, "Help me, I need you!" What was happening in your life that caused you to want to hit the reset button?

3. Many situations can cause us to feel the need to fight for our life, whether it's sorrow in our soul, sickness in our body, or struggles with our spouse . . . to name just a few. What is a situation you are facing in which you need to fight for the best life God wants you to have? How have you been wrestling in this area?

Where are you seeing victory? Where are you feeling the battle is still raging?

4. There may be times when we feel like crumpling up in a ball, crying, and saying, "God, fix it for me!" Why do you think God often calls you to stay in the fight instead of just resolving the situation for you?

How does God want us to fight, wrestle, and participate with Him in the journey toward a better life?

5. Read **Ephesians 2:8–10**. What does Paul say in these verses about who we are and what God thinks about us?

   What do you think and do that reflects you agree with God? What do you think and do that indicates you don't really believe these things God says about you?

6. The word in Ephesians 2:10 translated as *handiwork* (NIV) or *workmanship* (NKJV) carries the sense of a beautiful and elegant work of art fashioned by a master craftsman. Why is it often challenging to see ourselves the way that God does? What helps you believe and even declare that you are God's "masterpiece"?

7. As we walk through life, it always gets messy in the middle. We will all face times of pain, loss, and struggle. When this happens, we need to be ready to fight and wrestle our way through. What are you in the "middle" of right now?

How can your group members pray for you as you walk through this season?

8. Read **1 Peter 4:12–16** and **James 1:2–3**. The Bible is clear that living for Jesus does not guarantee a life free of struggle and pain. What are some appropriate ways we should respond when facing difficult, challenging times?

9. Read **Romans 1:20; Psalm 139:13–14;** and **Genesis 1:27**. In what ways were each of us made a masterpiece of God? Personally, how did this masterful work of God become even more amazing when you placed your faith in Jesus Christ?

10. Just as Joni Eareckson Tada went through the laborious process of learning how to paint using her teeth to hold a brush, we have to take risks, wrestle, and press on as God does His work within us. What is one way you need to "paint in a new way" even if it's not easy, simple, or quick? How can you begin to take a step of following Jesus today?

Closing Prayer

Use any of the following prompts to guide your group in a time of prayer:

- Thank God that His dreams and desires for your life are even better than what you can imagine.
- Praise God that when you are tired, weary, and ready to give up, He never gives up on you.
- Ask God to give you courage and strength to wrestle and fight for the life He wants to give you.
- Acknowledge to God that you understand (or long to understand) that you are His beautiful masterpiece. Thank Him for the good things He is growing in you.
- Lift up other members of your group and ask God to give them the strength they need to grow into the women of faith that He wants them to be.
- Ask God to help you talk with Him, sing His praises, and hold His hand tightly as you wrestle and face hard times in life.

BETWEEN-SESSIONS PERSONAL STUDY

Reflect on the content you've covered this week in *She's Still There* by engaging in any or all of the following between-sessions activities. The time you invest will be well spent, so let God use it to draw you closer to Him. At your next meeting, share with your group any key points or insights that stood out to you as you spent this time with the Lord.

Honest Evaluation

WHERE I AM . . . In this week's session, Chrystal describes how she hit a low point where she prayed, "God, break my legs!" Although she did not really want her legs broken, she was honestly crying out that she felt overwhelmed, underpowered, and at the end of her personal strength to press on. Find a quiet and private place, and spend a half-hour or so asking God to help you honestly assess your life: your heart, soul, relationships, and even your energy level. Write down what you feel God places on your heart or what rises to the surface during this time of reflection and prayer.

How is my soul right now?

How are my energy reserves?

Where am I presently wrestling?

Where do I need to begin wrestling?

HOW I GOT HERE . . . Consider your choices, your commitments, your daily schedule, and your decisions. What are some of the factors that got you to where you are today?

HOW I CAN RESET . . . What attitudes and outlooks do you need to change in your life? Where would you like to be? How do you feel God wants to change your life?

MY PLAN FOR WRESTLING . . . What are two or three actions you can begin today to help you engage, wrestle, and partner with God in moving toward the life He wants you to experience? Who can pray for you? How will you ask this person to both encourage you in your plan and hold you accountable?

If you choose to believe that you are defined only by your disappointments and disasters, you will abdicate your role in this world, the role that only you can play. But if you choose to embrace your journey—even the parts that disappoint you, challenge you, or make you double over from the emotional weight of it all—you can one day look back and see your hard [times] as a part of your life and not the definition of your life.

—*She's Still There*, page 30

Biblical Portraits

In this week's session, Chrystal noted there are many stories of people in the Bible who went through "messy times" as they fought to become the person whom God called them to be. Pick *one* such character from the following list and study his or her story in the passage provided. Then use the prompts provided to guide your reading and study.

- **Leah and Rachel:** Read Genesis 29–30
- **Joseph:** Genesis 39–40
- **Hannah:** Read 1 Samuel 1–2
- **David:** Read 2 Samuel 11–12; Psalm 41; and Psalm 51
- **Elijah:** Read 1 Kings 18–19
- **Esther:** Read Esther 3–4
- **Job:** Read Job 1–3
- **Shadrach, Meshach, and Abednego:** Read Daniel 3
- **Daniel:** Read Daniel 6
- **Mary:** Read Matthew 1–2 and Luke 1–2
- **Peter:** Read Luke 22:56–62 and Acts 12
- **Paul:** Read Acts 9 and 2 Corinthians 11–12

Study their story. What were they facing? What was their season of life? How was God present and at work in their lives?

Identify their struggle. What was their specific struggle? What was its source?

Look at how they responded. In what ways did this biblical character wrestle and fight for his or her life? How was God at work? What can you learn from this person's journey that will help you when you need to fight for your own life?

Be brave enough to believe you were made for more. Be bold enough to believe that healing can take place and that change is possible. And change is always possible. Even if your circumstances can't change, your attitude toward them can. Dare to trust that it's God's desire for you to live out a beautiful story designed with you in mind.

—*She's Still There*, page 43

Declare It!

MEMORIZE A PASSAGE OF SCRIPTURE. God's Word is always true, and the Bible says that you are a masterpiece. You might not believe it, and you might even dare to disagree with God on this particular topic, but you are wrong! Even when you don't recognize it or feel like it, you are a wonderful, beautiful, unique work of art crafted by none other than God Himself. With this truth in mind, take time in the coming days to memorize one of the following passages. If you feel motivated to do so, you might want to memorize more than one!

Ephesians 2:10
For we are God's handiwork, created in Christ Jesus to do good works, which God prepared in advance for us to do.

Psalm 139:13–14

For you created my inmost being; you knit me together in my mother's womb. I praise you because I am fearfully and wonderfully made; your works are wonderful, I know that full well.

1 Peter 2:9

But you are a chosen people, a royal priesthood, a holy nation, God's special possession, that you may declare the praises of him who called you out of darkness into his wonderful light.

DECLARE IT IN THE GOOD TIMES AND IN THE MESSY MIDDLE! Read these passages and personalize them ("I am God's handiwork . . ." "I am fearfully and wonderfully made . . ." "I am God's special possession . . ."). Put these passages in your phone, write them on a card that you keep in your purse, or tape them on your fridge or the mirror in the bathroom. Declare them often and with confidence. Repeat them in your heart and with your lips until you agree with God and can declare who you are: His beloved child who has been saved by the grace of Jesus!

CHOOSE TO TRUST. Write a short prayer of trust in God. Let Him know that you believe His Word and that you know He never lies. Declare that you will trust that what He says about you is true, even when you can't see it or fully understand it. Tell God that you will grow to see yourself the way He does—both in the good times and even the messy middle times of life.

There is always an anatomy to our drifts. We didn't meander miles away in a minute. Slowly and gradually we took steps, possibly unconsciously, that took us farther than we intended. However, if we pause to examine our drifts and see them for what they are—small abdications over time—we realize that we do indeed have the power to change. We can know that our drift is not as big, overpowering, or insurmountable as it seems. Here's the good news. If there is a way in, there is a way out. While you may feel utterly lost, take comfort in this: lost does not equal lifeless. And as long as there is still life, there is hope.

—*She's Still There*, page 52

Recommended Reading

As you reflect on what God is teaching you through this session, review chapters 1–5 in *She's Still There* and use the space provided to write any key points or questions you want to bring to the next group meeting. In preparation for your next session, read chapters 6–11.

LOOK AT YOUR LIFE

It is your job in this life to know and value what makes you *you* and to treasure the opportunity you have to make a distinct impression with this one life you have. No one else can do this for you. Sure, other people might encourage you, call things out of you, or help you along the way by lighting your path, but the responsibility of carrying your contents carefully is yours. Never forget, my friend, that your God-given life is yours to live.

Chrystal Evans Hurst

Opening Reflection

The ocean is beautiful, majestic, and breathtaking. A drive along any coast or a short boat ride will make this powerfully clear. People comment, almost reflexively, about the grandeur and magnificence of these massive bodies of water made by the Master Creator.

But the truth is that most people have never truly seen the full splendor of the ocean. Most of us have only driven by the ocean along the coast, or stood on a beach watching the waves roll in, or skimmed over the water on a boat. If you want to see the amazing colors, creativity, and staggering beauty of the ocean, you have to plunge deep.

If you have ever gone snorkeling or scuba diving, you have seen a whole other world. Schools of fish swim by, dazzling the eye with colors reserved for this underwater world. Coral, ocean plants, and creatures of rare shapes and sizes live in this hidden domain. There is far more to see under the water than there is to see on top of it. But the only way to open your eyes to these precious sights is to slow down, dive deep, and look closely.

Much of life is like this. We think we see the best and most beautiful in our world, other people, and even ourselves, but we are often just skimming the surface. It is only when we take a deep breath, plunge in, and open our eyes that we see more lovely and exquisite things than we ever dreamed of before. It is only when we stop to really *look* at our lives that we notice the beauty of our unique gifts, abilities, interests, and nature that God has given us.

We are all recipients of this "precious cargo" from God. The question is whether we are taking the time to wake up and appreciate all the blessings that He has provided. For it is only when we recognize our own gifts that we are able to act on the opportunities God places in our path each day to use them—and then, in turn, bless others.

Talk About It

To get things started for this second session, discuss one of the following questions:

- Tell about a time you were entrusted with caring for something of value. What did you do to protect that thing?

    or

- Tell about a time you were given something but didn't immediately recognize it had value in your life. What served as your "wake up call" to recognize its value?

Video Teaching Notes

Play the video segment for session two. As you watch, use the following outline to record any thoughts or concepts that stand out to you.

God made you *physically* unique, but you are also unique from a soul standpoint. No one has your specific personality, aspirations, dreams, creativity, attitude, or outlook . . . even your signature is different from others.

If you "fall asleep at the wheel" by not recognizing your gifts, you not only lose out on the opportunity to participate with God in what He wants to do but also on the opportunity to place your unique imprint on the end result.

You are born not only with a physical body but also with a *soul*. The degree to which you allow the Spirit of God to fill your soul determines the level of connectivity you will have with Him.

Everything that happens in life affects the "starter soul" you were given at birth and may change the shape of it. You pay attention to the shape your soul is in by recognizing your:

- **G**ifts

- **A**bilities

- **I**nterests

- **N**ature

You have to take the time to stop and recognize the gifts, abilities, interests, and nature that God has given you. It is only when you recognize these strengths within you that you are able to know how to use them to serve others and glorify God in the process.

Don't get so engrossed in the business of just living life that you forget to invite the Spirit of God into your soul to do His work. You can only be used to the fullness of God's intention when you allow the living Spirit of God to "fuel" your life.

Pay attention to the gifts God has given to you, take care of your body and soul, and then look for the little opportunities God provides each day to use your gifts for His glory. Don't get so caught up in "finding your purpose" that you miss these opportunities in life.

It's important to allow the Spirit of God to fill you each day so you can fully express the best of the unique gifts that God has given to you while on this earth.

Bible Study and Group Discussion

Take a few minutes with your group members to discuss what you just watched and explore these concepts in Scripture.

1. When was a time you slowed down and noticed something beautiful or wonderful that you had not really seen before? Or when was a time you noticed something good and beautiful in yourself and were surprised by this precious cargo God placed in you?

2. Read **Psalm 139:1–16**. What does this passage say about your *constituency* and your *destiny*? What can you know about yourself and about God by reading this psalm?

3. Read **Genesis 2:7** and **Jeremiah 1:4–5**. What do these passages teach about when God's plan for His people begins? What kind of a plan does He have for us?

4. What is something unique about you (such as your personality, physical traits, dreams, creativity, culture, or habits) that people in your group might not know about? How does this distinctive trait help make you who you are?

5. Read **1 Corinthians 6:19–20**. Why is it important to make wise and godly decisions in terms of what we do with our bodies? What is one way you could take a positive step forward in caring for your body out of respect for the God who made you?

6. How would you describe the condition of your soul right now? How is your soul healthy and in good shape? How is your soul hurting and in need of care?

7. Read **Jeremiah 31:3**; **Isaiah 43:2–4**; and **Luke 12:6–7**. What do we learn from these passages about how God cares for our souls? Why should this impact the way we view and care for our souls?

8. God has given each of us unique gifts, abilities, interests, and natures. Together they form the acronym *GAIN*. Take a moment to write down two or three examples of how each of these is uniquely growing in you:

    •   Gifts (things you are naturally good at)

- Abilities (things you have worked at to develop in yourself)

- Interests (things you are passionate about)

- Nature (your personality)

Share one of these items with your group members. Describe what you like about it and how it makes you uniquely who God has designed you to be. Talk about how you can use that specific trait to bring glory to God.

9. Read **Galatians 5:16–18** and **Ephesians 5:15–20**. How does the Spirit of God help us take care of our bodies and take care of our souls? What are some practical ways you can invite the Holy Spirit to work in you at a deeper level?

10. What strengths have you forgotten, walked away from, or dismissed about yourself that God wants you to take time to look at and restore? What steps can you take to begin this restoration process?

Closing Prayer

Use any of the following prompts to guide your group in a time of prayer:

- Ask God to help you slow down and notice the precious things He has placed within you. Give Him praise for each of these traits.
- Thank God that He has been at work in you since you were in your mother's womb. Agree with Him that you are wonderfully made!
- Confess where you have ignored or even made little of the precious things that God has placed in you.
- Pray for the Spirit of God to fill you, guide you, and transform your body and soul.
- Ask the Holy Spirit to reveal when you drift or make poor decisions. Pray for Him to wake you up and get you back on the road.
- Commit, in prayer, to embrace and honor God with your gifts, abilities, interests, and your unique nature.
- Take turns thanking God for the gifts you see in other group members.

BETWEEN-SESSIONS PERSONAL STUDY

Reflect on the content you've covered this week in *She's Still There* by engaging in any or all of the following between-sessions activities. The time you invest will be well spent, so let God use it to draw you closer to Him. At your next meeting, share with your group any key points or insights that stood out to you as you spent this time with the Lord.

Getting to Know Me . . .

Psalm 139:1–16 provides a startling revelation of how well God knows you. Almost every verse reveals something about God and something about you. Take time to read, reflect, and journal through this psalm. Use the prompts and space provided to guide this learning exercise.

Verses 1–3: "You have searched me, LORD, and you know me. You know when I sit and when I rise; you perceive my thoughts from afar. You discern my going out and my lying down; you are familiar with all my ways."

What I learn about God:

What I learn about me:

How I should see myself:

An action I could take:

My prayer that I can walk in this truth:

Verses 4–5: "Before a word is on my tongue you, LORD, know it completely. You hem me in behind and before, and you lay your hand upon me."

What I learn about God:

What I learn about me:

How I should see myself:

An action I could take:

My prayer that I can walk in this truth:

Verses 7–10: "Where can I go from your Spirit? Where can I flee from your presence? If I go up to the heavens, you are there; if I make my bed in the depths, you are there. If I rise on the wings of the dawn, if I settle on the far side of the sea, even there your hand will guide me, your right hand will hold me fast."

What I learn about God:

What I learn about me:

How I should see myself:

An action I could take:

My prayer that I can walk in this truth:

Verses 11–12: "If I say, 'Surely the darkness will hide me and the light become night around me,' even the darkness will not be dark to you; the night will shine like the day, for darkness is as light to you."

What I learn about God:

What I learn about me:

How I should see myself:

An action I could take:

My prayer that I can walk in this truth:

Verses 13–14: "For you created my inmost being; you knit me together in my mother's womb. I praise you because I am fearfully and wonderfully made; your works are wonderful, I know that full well."

What I learn about God:

What I learn about me:

How I should see myself:

An action I could take:

My prayer that I can walk in this truth:

Verses 15–16: "My frame was not hidden from you when I was made in the secret place, when I was woven together in the depths of the earth. Your eyes saw my unformed body; all the days ordained for me were written in your book before one of them came to be."

What I learn about God:

What I learn about me:

How I should see myself:

An action I could take:

My prayer that I can walk in this truth:

It's not enough to know you are a unique, divinely created soul. You must believe it. And to believe it, you must choose to remember what you already know—or learn what you don't. Then you must choose to rehearse the idea of your value until it becomes so ingrained in your mind that it affects what you do, how you think, and the way you respond to what has occurred in your life, whether you caused it or not.

—*She's Still There*, page 79

God's Unique Creation

Of all that God has created, humans are the most unique. Everything about you makes you one-of-a-kind. Even identical twins are not identical! Take time to think about how God has uniquely made you. List some things that set you apart and make you exactly who God created you to be.

Ways I am unique physically:

Ways I am unique in my personality:

Ways I am unique in my habits and idiosyncrasies:

Ways I am unique in my creativity and dreams:

Ways I am unique in my outlooks and attitudes:

Write a prayer thanking God for the many ways He has formed you and shaped you. Ask Him to help you joyfully embrace who you are.

God expects us to discover, develop, and deploy our gifts as we live this life. While God gives us life, we honor Him by using what He's placed inside. We show appreciation when we develop our abilities and skills. We live fully when we make room for our interests and passions. And we gain clarity when we take stock of our nature—our personality, character, and temperament.

—*She's Still There*, page 91

Looking for Your Life

There are three key ways to look at your life and move forward in allowing the Holy Spirit to strengthen your body and grow your soul. Take time to reflect on each of these this week.

1. **Pay attention to what God has given you.** Ponder and reflect on all that God has given to you. List three things that you can easily identify:

   -
   -
   -

   Now list three things God has given you that you seem to forget or fail to notice on a regular basis:

   -
   -
   -

2. **Care for your body and soul.** List two ways that you can care for your body and two ways that you can nurture your soul in the coming weeks.

   Care for your body:
   -
   -

   Care for your soul:
   -
   -

3. **Pay attention to heavenly hints.** Take time in the coming week to notice and list "heavenly hints" that God leaves to help you see who you are and who you are meant to be.

   -
   -
   -

You are a soul that functions in a spiritual way, designed to be fully alive only when you are filled to overflowing with life that bubbles up with the Spirit of God. There is no one like you, and you have the power of the God of all yesterdays and today and forever who is willing to help you. But without the living Spirit of God operating in and through your one-of-a-kind life, you can function, but your life will not have power. . . . Without the power of God operating in your life, you cannot have a useful and fruitful life and participate in His plans.

—*She's Still There*, page 102

Recommended Reading

As you reflect on what God is teaching you through this session, review chapters 6–11 in *She's Still There* and use the space provided to write any key points or questions you want to bring to the next group meeting. In preparation for your next session, read chapters 12–15.

EMBRACE YOUR LIFE

Your pain is a part of the process that leads to the girl inside you living her life. The pain that carves out pieces of your heart is the same pain that creates space in your soul to love with more compassion, live with greater wisdom, and experience an unexpectedly full, deep, and overwhelming joy. Rescuing the girl in you means embracing all of you, even the painful parts.

Chrystal Evans Hurst

Opening Reflection

When the church started a mentoring program for women, Angela signed up right away. She was facing a lot in life as a young woman, wife, and mother of three, and she knew the wisdom and prayer of a godly and mature woman would be valuable. The mentor whom Angela hoped she would get was Esther, a woman in her eighties, and one of the most mature and joyful people Angela had ever met. Angela prayed (and also discreetly mentioned to the mentoring ministry leader) that she would be honored to have Esther invest in her life.

To her delight, Angela was paired up with Esther, and they set a date for the first of many weekly "tea times," as Esther called them. Their time together began with prayer, and then Angela asked Esther one simple question from the list the church provided: "Could you tell me your story?" Little did Angela know that this question would take them through their entire tea time and into the next week, when they would meet again.

Angela had interacted with Esther many times at church and had been amazed by her deep sense of joy as they talked about faith and ministry. She had always assumed that Esther must have had a simple and smooth life because of that joyful spirit. But on this day Angela learned that Esther, now a widow, had been married three times. Her first husband had died in the war. Her second husband had left her for another woman. Her third husband had died after a brief but painful battle with cancer.

Angela also learned Esther had three children. The middle child had died in a tragic drowning accident in her twenties. Esther said, "There are not many days that I don't think of her, see her face in my mind, and miss her."

Indeed, Esther had not walked an easy path. She had experienced many wonderful moments, but also many times of deep and painful loss—and it had all been a part of the work that God had done in her life. The same is true for us. In order to recover the girl we saw in the mirror—the one we know is *still there*—we have to embrace both the joy and the pain as part of the work God is doing in us.

Talk About It

To get things started for this third session, discuss one of the following questions:

- Have you ever skipped ahead to the last pages of a book to see how things turned out? What might we miss when we skip pages or chapters of a book and try to get to the ending too quickly?

or

- Tell about a time when you dropped out of a healthy-eating regimen or exercise program because it was difficult, and describe any regret you felt because you did this.

Video Teaching Notes

Play the video segment for session three. As you watch, use the following outline to record any thoughts or concepts that stand out to you.

Giving birth to anything worthwhile means embracing *all* parts of the process—both the joyful *and* painful parts. If you jump past any part, you miss out on what God wants to do in you.

The journey to sanctification is just as important as where you will be one day in heaven. God delights in the details—He loves the *steps*—that will get you to the end result.

You show you are embracing your life when you have *pep in your step*. You choose to walk with energy and excitement along your journey, looking for the simple joys that fill you up.

You embrace the "good stuff" and nourish your soul through . . .

- Your senses

- Your significance (relationships)

- The Spirit of God

You embrace your life when you recognize *purpose in each step*. There is purpose in the pain you have experienced—it tells you about the construct of your soul.

Embracing your life also involves *staying in step*. You need to be faithful to keep going in the process that God has set before you. Each and every step matters.

You are never fighting *for* victory but *from* victory. Your job is to live well one step at a time, fully embracing what you do know, what you can do, and who you can be today.

Finally, embracing your life means being willing to *step higher when it's time*. Build on the gifts that God has given to you and trust Him when He tells you to move.

Bible Study and Group Discussion

Take a few minutes with your group members to discuss what you just watched and explore these concepts in Scripture.

1. Think about some painful experiences that you have faced. How did those experiences drain and discourage you? How did they shape your soul and grow your faith?

2. Now think about a painful experience you went through that actually holds fond memories for you because the end result was a blessing (for example, running a 10K or experiencing childbirth). How did you forget the pain and focus on the positive?

3. What is a challenge you are going through right now that you need to embrace and learn to find joy in the journey? How can your group members support and pray for you as you walk through this process?

4. Read **Psalm 37:23–24**; **Philippians 2:12–16**; and **2 Corinthians 3:17–18**. What do these passages teach about how God uses a process to shape us over time into the people He wants us to be?

What problems might we face when we look for instant change and immediate results in terms of our spiritual growth and maturity?

5. Read **Ecclesiastes 3:12–13**; **5:18–20**; and **9:7–10**. How do you respond to the outlook on life you find in these passages? How can you learn to take deeper enjoyment in these kinds of simple pleasures in life?

6. You are responsible for nourishing the growth and health of your soul. What are some simple ways you can strengthen your soul through . . .

   • Engaging your **senses**?

   • Engaging in **significant** relationships?

   • Engaging the **Spirit of God** through meaningful spiritual disciplines?

7. Read **Psalm 147:3**; **Matthew 11:28–30**; and **Romans 8:28**. What promises from God do these verses contain about the bitter seasons of life we will all endure?

8. We will all be tempted to give up and stop pressing on when the journey gets hard and we feel weary. What are some costs and consequences we might face if we give up and get out of step with the Lord during the hard times of life?

If you are willing to be vulnerable, share about a time you got out of step and stopped following God because things got hard. What did God do to help you get back in step with His plan and will for your life?

9. As we saw in the last session, the Bible is filled with people who pressed on and followed God even when they were not sure where they were going. What helps you keep following Jesus and pressing on even when you feel discouraged and don't see progress on your journey?

10. Read **Luke 16:10–12**; **Colossians 3:15–17**; and **1 Timothy 4:11–14**. God wants to call you to a higher level of devotion, faithfulness, and fruitfulness. What is one way He has been calling you to step up and live for Him with greater passion and commitment? How can your group members help you on this journey?

Closing Prayer

Use any of the following prompts to guide your group in a time of prayer:

- Ask God to help you see the path He has planned for you. Then, ask for courage to walk on this path, even when it's rocky and hard.
- Praise God for some of the specific things He is doing in your life that bring you joy.
- Pray for eyes to see the joy and blessings in the hard things you experience.
- Confess where you have not fully developed a specific gift that God has given to you and pray for power to grow in that gift for the glory of God.
- Pray that the group members would be intentional about seeking the filling of the Holy Spirit in their lives.

BETWEEN-SESSIONS PERSONAL STUDY

Reflect on the content you've covered this week in *She's Still There* by engaging in any or all of the following between-sessions activities. The time you invest will be well spent, so let God use it to draw you closer to Him. At your next meeting, share with your group any key points or insights that stood out to you as you spent this time with the Lord.

Learning from the Past

We all know that looking back and learning from past life lessons is a sign of maturity and wisdom. So today, take time to remember a past journey you walked through that took time, included pain, and that God used for His glory and your good.

What was the journey you went through that was difficult but life-giving?

How long did this journey last, or how long has it lasted if you are still in it?

What painful moments did you face on this journey?

What good things came out of this journey—lessons learned, faith deepened, increased level of spiritual maturity?

I hate to tell you this, but your pain, however it came about, is a part of your journey. You don't have to want to relive, remember, or rejoice over it, but it is a part of who you are. Your pain affects how you see the world and therefore how you see yourself. It's a part of your experience, the stuff God has allowed to impact your soul. So if you want to fully live your life, you must be willing to embrace your pain. Your quest to rescue your life will require your labor of love.

—*She's Still There*, pages 132–133

Simple Joys in Life

Use the following prompts to help you see the simple joys God has made available to you.

People you delight to spend time with:

Entertainment you enjoy:

Foods that you savor:

Activities that bring you life and places you love to go:

Other things that bring you joy:

Use this list as a reminder of things you can do to boost the joy quotient in your life. Make sure you are finding joy by engaging in these sorts of things on a regular basis!

Choose joy by way of the senses, significance, and the Spirit. Don't reach the end of your life or arrive at your goal and realize you were too focused on the result to enjoy the journey. It's the path to your purpose that holds the real joy. If you want to live a life worth remembering, you must slow down and pay attention. It's the only way to see and appreciate all the beauty in and around you . . . and there is plenty of beauty to be seen in everyday life.

—*She's Still There*, page 128

Offering God What You Have

Read the amazing account of Jesus feeding the five thousand in John 6:1–15. What are some key points that you notice in this passage?

The disciples could not see a way to feed all the people, but a young boy offered his snack lunch to Jesus as an act of faith. What contrast do you see between the disciples and the boy?

Do you truly believe God is big enough to take your abilities, offerings, and acts of faithfulness (no matter how small they seem to you) and multiply them for his glory? Write down five small things you could surrender to God in a fresh new way today:

-
-
-
-
-

Prayerfully ask the Lord to show you what specific things you can offer him in the coming days. Pray that he will take these offerings in his hands, bless them, and multiply them for his glory.

Do what you can with what you have. Your job is to live well, embracing what you do know, what you can do, and who you can be—today. If you wait until you have enough information or ability, the perfect opportunity or circumstances, or exactly the right mood, mindset, or physical makeup, you're pushing pause on your life.

She's Still There, page 143

Recommended Reading

As you reflect on what God is teaching you through this session, review chapters 12–15 in *She's Still There* and use the space provided to write any key points or questions you want to bring to the next group meeting. In preparation for your next session, read chapters 16–21.

DEVELOP YOUR LIFE

You will have to dig deep to make decisions that are sometimes
hard in order to head in directions that sometimes seem scary,
to exercise discipline that doesn't always feel good, and to use
discernment to operate in an environment that can keep you from
your focus. . . . I don't know what digging deep will look like in
your life, with the decisions that you must make to honor
the life of the girl in you, but I do know that you will
have to focus to do it. There is no other way.

Chrystal Evans Hurst

Opening Reflection

The boxes arrived on Steve and Patricia's doorstep three days before Christmas. The packages were prominently marked with Amazon labels, and Steve made sure he moved them to the garage before Patricia got home. It was her Christmas present—a beautiful desk and file cabinet set she had been admiring for months. She had no idea that Steve had caught on to how much she was hoping to get this desk, and he was excited to surprise her.

After dragging the bulky and heavy parcels to the garage, Steve opened them and set the contents on the floor. He was staggered and shocked by the number of pieces. He knew there was "Some Assembly Required" (hmmm) because the website had said so in a number of places. But as he faced the slats of wood, bags of hardware, and what seemed like more than a hundred individual pieces, he couldn't help feel get a bit overwhelmed. "I should have ordered this a month earlier," he muttered to himself.

Steve told Patricia not to come into the garage for the next few days. She agreed, and he got to work at 9:00 that night. The instructions were complex and hard to follow, so Steve decided to go with his gut and rely on his natural building ability to put the desk together. After pulling two consecutive all-nighters, he finally got the project finished. But he was concerned to find twenty-two pieces of hardware still lying on the garage floor. There were screws, bolts, small wooden pieces he could not identify, and even two little nobs.

Steve put these parts into a bag and tossed them on an upper shelf in the garage. When it came time to move the desk into the house on Christmas morning, he was irritated to find it was a bit wobbly. It did not feel like the "solid" and "high quality furniture" the advertisement had promised. As Steve looked at the bag of "extra stuff" that he had not used, he wondered if he had rushed the job and would have been wiser to follow the instructions.

But . . . it was Christmas now, and too late to go back and start over.

Talk About It

To get things started for this fourth session, discuss one of the following questions:

- Tell about a time you ignored the directions for something you were making or building, and describe what you learned from the experience.

or

- Tell about a lesson you learned after a person gave you some good advice but you failed to follow through on it.

Video Teaching Notes

Play the video segment for session four. As you watch, use the following outline to record any thoughts or concepts that stand out to you.

Participating with God in an effort to bring out the best in you requires *focus*. You have to choose to dig deep, develop your life, and focus on the finish line.

Paul was highly educated, trained as a Jewish rabbi, by birth a Roman citizen, and had access to everything needed to be a "good" person. He lived all-out for Jesus after his conversion and spread the gospel. Yet he said he was still working on developing his life.

The Christian walk is a lifelong process. It is part of your journey as a Christian to keep pressing forward and not "arrive" until you meet Jesus at the end of your life.

None of us like to stay in the "training" stage. But constant training is required for you to continue progressing at the rate God wants you to progress toward maturity in Christ.

There are four steps you need to take if you want to move forward in developing your life:

1. *Make a decision that is tied to an action.* Remember it's not a real decision for change until it is accompanied by an action step.

2. *Be consistent and pay attention.* You can't focus on the finish line if you are continually being distracted from your goal.

3. *Exercise discernment in your life.* You do this by surrounding yourself with people who will support your decision and your direction.

4. *Seek to be disciplined in your decision.* Discipline is what keeps you moving toward the goal when you don't feel like going on.

If there is an area of life in which you struggle to maintain discipline, ask Christ for His help to get you into the rhythm of obedience, submission, and surrender. Discipline is simply choosing between what you want right now and what you want most later on.

God promises that as you seek Him in His Word and grow in spiritual maturity, self-control will develop as a fruit of the Spirit within you.

When the Spirit of God is at work in you, you can go further than your own abilities would normally allow.

Bible Study and Group Discussion

Take a few minutes with your group members to discuss what you just watched and explore these concepts in Scripture.

1. In the Bible, we read that God is always doing a transformative work in the lives of His children. But what is our role in the process? What is required for you to participate with God in becoming the person he wants you to be?

2. What will it look like for you to make the *decision* to run the race well in one or two of these areas of your life? How will you know you have finished the race well?

   • Your health:

   • Your marriage and family:

   • Your career (whether inside or outside the home):

   • Your friendships:

- Your finances:

- Your spiritual life:

Share these areas with your group and discuss what your life will look like if you keep your eyes on Jesus and follow Him well.

3. Read **Philippians 3:12–14**. Paul had followed Jesus for more than twenty years when he wrote these words. God had used him to establish churches, and he had suffered much as he served Christ. Yet he was clear that he had not yet arrived spiritually. What do you learn in this passage from Paul's attitude, drive, and commitment?

4. It's important to push forward in the process of our spiritual development, but we also need to give ourselves a break and recognize this will be a lifelong journey. Why is it important to extend grace to ourselves along the way as we encounter hard times and occasionally get stuck? How does God express grace to us during these times?

5. Read **Luke 9:57–62**. Following Christ requires keeping our *attention* on Him. How did Jesus respond to the individuals in this passage who wanted to follow Him but had some conditions? What does this say about what is involved in truly following Jesus?

    In what areas are you tempted to lose focus and stop paying attention as you seek to live for Jesus? What are some things that are holding you back or standing in the way of you moving to the next step?

6. Staying true to our spiritual development will require us to *discern* what situations and people tend to get us off track. Read **Philippians 3:15–20**. Who is someone in your life who has provided a good example of making God-honoring decisions? What have you learned from this person's example as it relates to spiritual discipline?

7. What are some of the places and environments in your life that can shove you off the path, cause you to lose focus, and hinder your spiritual development? How can you avoid those situations, environments, and even people?

8. Read **1 Corinthians 9:24–27; 2 Timothy 1:7;** and **Hebrews 6:1–3.** Why is it so essential to exercise spiritual *discipline* in our lives? What will help us stay focused and disciplined when we feel tired, weary, and worn out?

9. Think about a specific time in your life when you exercised discipline and, through the power of the Holy Spirit, were able to succeed at something you thought was beyond your abilities to accomplish. How were you able to stay disciplined? What did you learn about yourself that you took into the next difficult situation you faced?

10. So . . . what decision will you make today to move toward becoming the person God wants you to be? Share with your group what goals you plan to establish. How can your group members support you, cheer you on, and provide accountability to help you stay disciplined in this area of your personal growth?

Closing Prayer

Use any of the following prompts to guide your group in a time of prayer:

- Thank God that He is gracious in laying out a path for His children. Ask Him for eyes to see the path He has for you with even greater clarity.
- Invite the Holy Spirit to fill you with power to make it to the finish line, every day, and for all of your life.
- Ask for discipline and discernment as you seek to develop a life that honors Jesus and reveals God's presence to others.
- Confess where you feel paralyzed and ask God to help you trust Him and get moving again.
- Thank God for the people He has put in your life to help you reach the goals He has for you.
- Pray for your group members to grow in their commitment to develop lives that honor Jesus and bring Him glory.

BETWEEN-SESSIONS PERSONAL STUDY

Reflect on the content you've covered this week in *She's Still There* by engaging in any or all of the following between-sessions activities. The time you invest will be well spent, so let God use it to draw you closer to Him. At your next meeting, share with your group any key points or insights that stood out to you as you spent this time with the Lord.

Life Development Plan

We are partners with God! He is always the senior partner, but He wants us to do our part. For this activity, use the space provided to create a life development plan using the steps that Chrystal outlined in this week's session. Once you have this area moving forward in a healthy way, consider adding another area in which you can partner with God to develop your life.

DECISION: Identify one specific area of your life that you know God wants you to develop and grow. Ask the Holy Spirit to guide you in this process. Once you have identified the area, purpose in your heart, with the strength of Jesus, to press forward in growth.

DIRECTION: It is not enough to simply identify an area and decide to do it. You need to also set a direction for the steps you will take to get there. Write down actions you need to take (and actions you need to stop) if you are going to grow in this area of your life.

- Actions to take:

- Actions to stop:

DISCERNMENT: Recognize there will be obstacles that will threaten to get in the way of your progress in developing the life God wants for you (and that you want for yourself). List two or three possible roadblocks or stumbling blocks that you might confront. Then identify how you can avoid those barriers to keep pressing forward.

- Possible roadblocks:

• How I can avoid these roadblocks:

DISCIPLINE: Finally, you will need to press on even when it gets hard. What will help you keep focused, on task, and moving forward even when you feel like quitting? Lay out one or two strategies that will help you keep on task in this specific area:

Some decision is better than no decision even if the decision you can make today is small. And don't despise the small things. Doing something that might seem insignificant is still doing something. Don't undermine your efforts by ignoring the one small thing you can do to move from thought to action. Small movements still contribute to momentum.

—*She's Still There*, page 172

Learning from Fellow Travelers

One of the best ways to persevere in the journey of developing your life is to look at those who have gone before you and pressed on through the hard times. Take a few moments to learn from one biblical character (the apostle Paul) and one modern example (of your choosing).

BIBLICAL EXAMPLE: Read the following passages of Scripture and write down what you learn from the apostle Paul about standing strong and following Jesus even during the hard times.

Acts 16:16–40

2 Corinthians 11:16–33

Philippians 3:10–21

MODERN EXAMPLE: Consider pairing up with another member of your group sometime during the week. Identify one Christian you both know and respect who has stood strong and continued to develop his or her life even in the face of trials and struggles. Contact this person and ask the following questions, keeping notes of the lessons you learn in the "interview."

What are some of the struggles, trials, and pain you have faced in your life?

What has God taught you through these hard times?

What has helped you to stay disciplined, continuing to press on when you felt like quitting or giving up?

What wisdom would you give me as I seek to continue developing my life and following Jesus through the hard times I face?

You need to surround yourself with people who get where you're trying to go—people who can support you, join you, or give you some direction. If there are people in your life who don't do any of the above, it's your job to decide the amount of influence they have in your life—or whether they should be in your life at all. Yes. It's that serious.

—*She's Still There*, page 189

Commit It to Memory

The Word of God can provide you with discernment and discipline when you need encouragement as you seek to grow in spiritual maturity in Christ. With this in mind, commit the following passages to memory during the coming week. Keep them in your phone, posted on the fridge, or on a mirror you look into regularly.

Philippians 3:13–14

Brothers and sisters, I do not consider myself yet to have taken hold of it. But one thing I do: Forgetting what is behind and straining toward what is ahead, I press on toward the goal to win the prize for which God has called me heavenward in Christ Jesus.

1 Corinthians 9:24

Do you not know that in a race all the runners run, but only one gets the prize? Run in such a way as to get the prize.

Discipline is the habit of acting in the moment based on a decision you made in advance, regardless of your feelings. It's the action that bridges the gap between your dreams and your reality. Discipline is the sinew that connects your decision, your direction, and the discernment you must use each and every day. It binds you by your will—not your emotions or the circumstances of any given day. And most important, discipline is what gets you going again when you've screwed up, dropped the ball, or gotten off course.

—*She's Still There*, pages 202–203

Recommended Reading

As you reflect on what God is teaching you through this session, review chapters 16–21 in *She's Still There* and use the space provided to write any key points or questions you want to bring to the next group meeting. In preparation for your next session, read chapters 22–25.

ENCOURAGE YOUR LIFE

If focus is central—the hub in the wheel that moves your life forward—then your decisions, direction, discernment, and discipline are the spokes—your efforts to set things in motion. But what it takes to start making progress is not always enough to keep making progress. Like a wheel, the hub of your life also needs a rim. Your ability to coach yourself is that rim. It is good to have people in your life who cheer you on or give you guidance, but you must be willing to encourage yourself so you can keep your momentum going.

Chrystal Evans Hurst

Opening Reflection

Almost every sports team has a coach of some kind. Children's soccer teams . . . basketball teams . . . gymnastics teams . . . cheerleading teams . . . and just about every other team you can imagine has a person with this specific job and role. And if you have ever sat on a bleacher or in a folding chair on the sidelines of a game, you have undoubtedly realized there are all kinds of coaches. Maybe you have seen one of these:

- **The Encourager:** These coaches are filled with joy. They always have a kind word to say; they see the best in their athletes; and they let them know what they do well. These coaches might not even know much about the game, but they love their players and cheer them on with a positive, uplifting spirit. Kids who play for such a coach will often feel positive about themselves and the experience.

- **The Teacher:** Some coaches focus on skills, rules, and the nuances of the sport. They are quick to give instruction to their athletes, like to explain how to play the game, and are helpful in teaching strategy. Children who have a coach like this learn a great deal, understand the game, and can become masters of strategy.

- **The Screamer:** Unfortunately, there are also coaches who believe that yelling is the best way to get the most out of their teams. They "motivate" their players by screaming at them (or the referees) when a mistake is made or a call doesn't go their way. Children who play for these coaches usually end up feeling discouraged and disinterested in the sport.

- **The Critic:** Then there are those coaches who seem to feel their job is to point out what their players are doing wrong. They know a great deal about the sport and expect their players to know as much as they do. Children who play on a team with a coach like this will tend to feel bad about their skills—and maybe even about who they are as a person.

The truth is that we are *all* coaches in one way or another. While we might not be coaching a sports team, we still coach ourselves every day of our lives. The question is not *whether* we coach ourselves, but what *kind* of coach we are to ourselves.

Talk About It

To get things started for this fifth session, discuss one of the following questions:

- If you have ever played for a coach who fell into one of these categories, how did that experience affect your feelings toward the game?

or

- What are some ways that you "coach yourself" in life? Which of the above categories do you tend to fall into when you do this?

Video Teaching Notes

Play the video segment for session five. As you watch, use the following outline to record any thoughts or concepts that stand out to you.

Your mind can run away and cause you not to function when you fail to take your thoughts captive, coach your heart, or operate in a way that falls in line with the truth of God's Word.

In the psalms, we see that when things were at their worst for David, he was able to "coach himself" through the situation by focusing on the truth of the God he served.

The first way to coach yourself is with your *lips*. Be nurturing with the words you say to yourself and recognize they have power in your life.

The second way to coach yourself is with your head (or *mind)*. Chase down those loose thoughts that are not going in the right direction, lasso them, and take them captive.

There are three ways that you can win the battle in your mind:

1. **Encourage:** receiving a "nudge" at times to pursue healthy thoughts

2. **Examine:** writing out your thoughts to recognize if they are truth

3. **Expose:** placing yourself around people who have a positive influence on you

The third way to coach yourself is with your *heart*. Take the time to root out the issues in your heart that are festering and can cause greater pain later.

The fourth way to coach yourself is with your *hands*. Be willing to not only look at your thoughts but also take action to correct any wrong thoughts.

You cannot make God any bigger than He already is, but you can magnify or diminish your perspective of Him by what you choose to rehearse in your heart and mind.

Bible Study and Group Discussion

Take a few minutes with your group members to discuss what you just watched and explore these concepts in Scripture.

1. Read **1 Samuel 30:1–6**. What situation were the Israelites facing? What caused them to "weep aloud"? What personal crises was David facing in this situation?

2. In response to this dire situation, David "found strength in the LORD his God." What are some of the ways you have learned to find strength or encouragement in the Lord?

3. Read **Proverbs 12:18**; **18:21** and **James 3:6–10**. What do these passages teach about the power of our words? How do you think these passages should impact the way we speak to ourselves about ourselves?

4. How have you experienced the goodness of words that bless and heal? How have you experienced the burn and pain of words that hurt and damage?

5. **Read Romans 12:1–2; 2 Corinthians 10:3–5; and Philippians 4:8–9.**
    What do these passages teach about the importance of what we think and how
    we coach our minds? What dangers will we face if wrong and false thoughts
    dominate our thinking?

6. As we saw in this week's video, there are three practical ways to coach our head
    and transform our thinking. Identify with your group at least two to three
    practical ways you can put these into practice.

    • **Encourage:** How can you stay positive and affirm yourself even when you are
      in the midst of a struggle?

    • **Examine:** How can you examine your inner dialogue and uncover the deceit
      the enemy has rooted in your mind?

    • **Expose:** What are ways you can flood your mind with right thinking and
      truth?

7. Read **Proverbs 3:5–6**; **4:23** and **Jeremiah 17:9–10**. What does the Bible teach about the importance of guarding our hearts and knowing what resides within them?

8. How can our lives get out of control when we allow our emotions to go unchecked? What are some ways to submit your heart to God's truth so it will not rule your decisions and your life?

9. Read **James 1:22–25**. Why is it essential for our faith to move from our head and our heart into our hands and our feet? What is wrong with a faith that is all about beliefs but never moves us to action?

10. As you coach your lips, head, heart, and hands, what are some of the actions you want to see become natural for you? How can your group members pray for you and encourage you as you seek to put your faith into action in this specific area?

Closing Prayer

Use any of the following prompts to guide your group in a time of prayer:

- Thank God for the people in your life who have modeled great self-coaching.
- Pray for discipline to read the Bible daily so that you can let the words of God become the words you speak to encourage yourself.
- Ask the Holy Spirit to guard your mind (and the minds of your small-group members) from the lies of the enemy and the cruel messages of the world.
- Invite the Lord to heal the parts of your heart that have been damaged by the lies that you have been told.
- Consecrate your hands and life to God in a fresh new way. Tell God that you are ready to serve Him and care for others.
- Lift up words of blessing to God as David did in Psalm 34. Begin your prayer with the words, "I will extol the LORD at all times, his praise will always be on my lips" (verse 1). Continue with a declaration of praise and worship to God.

BETWEEN-SESSIONS PERSONAL STUDY

Reflect on the content you've covered this week in *She's Still There* by engaging in any or all of the following between-sessions activities. The time you invest will be well spent, so let God use it to draw you closer to Him. At your next meeting, share with your group any key points or insights that stood out to you as you spent this time with the Lord.

Examine Your Mind

This week, Chrystal noted one of the ways you win the battle in your mind is by *examining* your thoughts to determine if you are believing lies, and then to speak God's truth to yourself. Take a few minutes to reflect on a difficult situation you are facing and how you are encouraging yourself through it. Ask the Holy Spirit to uplift you as you respond to the following prompts.

One situation I am facing today that is discouraging or difficult is:

I know this is true about myself as I face this situation:

I know this is true about God's greatness as I face this situation:

I know this is true about God's character as I face this situation:

I know this is true about God's faithfulness in the past as I face this situation:

Spend some time meditating on these truths, thanking God for revealing them to you, and letting His truth encourage your soul!

Speaking life to your heart and to your situation may mean speaking God's truth out loud as you look yourself in the eye. Speaking life simply means speaking kindly to yourself and encouraging yourself just like you would a good friend. And it's worth learning to be your own best friend, even if it means talking to yourself out loud every now and again.

—*She's Still There*, page 224

Examine Your Heart

Once you have identified the false ideas that are rattling around in your head, you have to replace them in your *heart* with God's truth. Write down five little or big lies that you have noticed are affecting your heart.

LIES THAT LIVE IN MY HEAD

1.	
2.	
3.	
4.	
5.	

Now, look up the following passages of Scripture and, in your own words, write down the truth of what God says to you.

TRUTH GOD WANTS ME TO KNOW

Psalm 139:13–14
Matthew 6:26
Romans 8:17
Ephesians 2:10
1 Thessalonians 5:5
1 Peter 2:9

When you find yourself pondering the lie or even buying into it, replace it with the truth. Speak this truth, declare it, meditate on it, and cling to it!

Regardless of how we feel about what's happening in our lives, we need to learn how to interpret our emotions. Sometimes emotion comes suddenly. We realize after the fact that we have fallen into a pit and are now way under the ground. But many times, feelings engulf us gradually. Drifts often begin with emotions that, like strong currents, gradually carry us away. Our choice to coach ourselves through our emotions can either perpetuate the pit we find ourselves in or prevent us from sinking further.

—*She's Still There*, page 238

Expose Yourself to the Truth

Exposing yourself to the truth involves learning from the example of those who have successfully coached themselves in the face of difficulties. The Bible provides many such examples of people who acknowledged God's truth about themselves in the face of lies, conflict, and spiritual attack. During the coming week, study the life of one or two of the following examples from Scripture.

• **Joshua:** Read Joshua 1; 6; and 23

What do I learn from Joshua's example?

What specific changes can I make in how I coach myself because of what I learned?

- **David:** Read Psalms 3; 7; 9; and 11

What do I learn from David's example?

What specific changes can I make in how I coach myself because of what I learned?

- **Elisha:** Read 2 Kings 2; 4; and 6

What do I learn from Elisha's example?

What specific changes can I make in how I coach myself because of what I learned?

• **Paul:** Read Philippians 1; 3 and Acts 16

What do I learn from Paul's example?

What specific changes can I make in how I coach myself because of what I learned?

Coach yourself toward the girl in you. Identify your areas of focus and what steps you will take to move toward them. Decide how you will give those things priority. Build your schedule around them. Make time for them. Do less of other things so you can do more of the things you've decided will make a difference in your story. Check in regularly to assess your progress and, if you've gotten off track, do whatever is necessary to get it together and move on.

—*She's Still There*, page 252

Recommended Reading

As you reflect on what God is teaching you through this session, review chapters 22–25 in *She's Still There* and use the space provided to write any key points or questions you want to bring to the next group meeting. In preparation for your next session, read chapters 26–30.

CHOOSE YOUR LIFE

Freedom comes when you realize the person running next
to you can't run your race the way you can—nor you theirs.
Freedom is born when you commit to fighting your way to the
finish, because no one can claim your medal but you. Freedom
comes when you stop comparing yourself with the person ahead of
you or behind you and choose to have a healthy respect for yourself
as you put one foot in front of the other. Stop letting where
other people are in their run determine how you
feel about your own. Run your race.

Chrystal Evans Hurst

Opening Reflection

In 1980, at the eighty-fourth annual Boston Marathon, an entrant named Rosie Ruiz was the first woman to cross the finish line. Her time of 2:31:56 was the fastest in race history for a female runner and the third fastest ever recorded for a female athlete in any marathon. Most astounding, Rosie hardly seemed tired; she was barely sweating, despite the fact she did not appear to be in top athletic shape.

Rosie celebrated her victory with great joy. But then, eight days later, to the shock of the running world, the title was taken from her and given to Jacqueline Gareau, the second-place female finisher. It seems that race officials had become suspicious when Gareau, who had been leading the race at the seventeen-mile mark, said she never saw Rosie pass her. As the evidence mounted, it became clear that Rosie had cheated. Investigators found that she took the subway for part of the race and then jumped back on the course at the end.

Rosie had indeed qualified for the race and was a strong marathoner, but she knew there was no chance she could win the race on her own merits. Her desire to be a winner at all costs led her to choose to take the path of deception. The desire to be popular, loved, and successful can also drive us to do all sorts of things and pretend that we are someone else. It can cause us to put on masks, pretend, lie, and even deceive ourselves.

God's plan is to empower us to run our own race and choose to live our own lives. When we learn to do this, we will always be victorious, because winning means running the course God has set before us. If we try to run someone else's race, by definition, we have already lost!

Talk About It

To get things started for this sixth session, discuss one of the following questions:

- If you or someone you know have ever participated in a marathon or a race, what choices needed to be made to train for the event?

  or

- What are the dangers of being *too* competitive with others?

Video Teaching Notes

Play the video segment for session six. As you watch, use the following outline to record any thoughts or concepts that stand out to you.

Freedom occurs when you choose to run your own race, do the best you can do with what God has given you, and learn how to be satisfied with what you have.

The way you choose to respond to what the Holy Spirit is doing in your life will determine how well you run your race. The minute you try to run *someone else's* race, you will lose not only your race but also your freedom.

One way to choose freedom is to recognize what's good about your race and then *celebrate* it.

A second way to choose freedom is to not *compare* yourself to others.

A third way to choose freedom is to be *honest* with yourself.

A fourth way to choose freedom is to engage in *community*.

People choose to wear "masks" to protect themselves from the possibility of hurt. But the truth is that the masks will also prevent you from receiving the very thing you want the most.

Choose to believe it is possible to rescue the girl you once saw in the mirror. Believe that *she is still there*—and then fight to reclaim her!

Bible Study and Group Discussion

Take a few minutes with your group members to discuss what you just watched and explore these concepts in Scripture.

1.   Why is it so dangerous to spend our time and energy running someone else's race rather than choosing the life God has for us?

2.   Read **2 Corinthians 3:17–18**. How does being led by the Spirit of God and following God's will for your life lead to true freedom? How does following your own path in your own strength, or the path others pressure you to walk, lead to bondage?

3. Think about some of the ways you encourage, bless, and cheer on other women as they run their race and live for Jesus. What would happen if you were just as encouraging and positive with yourself as you are with them?

   Why is it easier to cheer others on and bless them than it is to encourage yourself?

4. Share one positive forward step you have taken on your race of faith and life the past week. How was God present? How do you think your heavenly Father feels about your forward progress (even when it is seemingly small to you)?

5. Read **Psalm 95:1–3** and **Colossians 3:17**. Why are thanksgiving, celebration, and gratitude so important as we run the race of life and faith?

What are some specific ways you can celebrate and express gratitude for your steps forward and ways that you are growing in spiritual maturity?

6. Read **Philippians 4:11–13; 1 Timothy 6:6–10;** and **Hebrews 13:5**. How does contentment set us free to run the race God has set before us? How does lack of contentment hold us back from reaching the goal?

7. What is one area of your life where you find it hard to be content? What good things do you have in this area that you can focus on, be thankful for, and celebrate?

8. Read **Proverbs 28:13; James 5:15–16;** and **1 John 1:5–10**. Why is it so important to confess our sins if we are going to run our race in freedom? How does unconfessed sin create bondage and keep us from moving forward on our journey with Jesus?

9. In what ways does having a trusted and mature sister in Christ (with whom you can be completely honest about your struggles) help you move forward in freedom? What does it take to become this kind of trusted and confident friend to another woman?

10. Read **Psalm 133:1–3; 1 Peter 3:8**; and **1 John 4:11–12**. How does walking in community with other women who love Jesus help you stay the course and run your race well?

How can your group members become a community of encouragement and inspiration to one another as you seek to become the woman God wants you to be?

Closing Prayer

Use any of the following prompts to guide your group in a time of prayer:

- Ask God to show you *your* race and then to help you focus on that race . . . not the race He has set for another person to run.
- Pray for wisdom to celebrate others as they run their race, and ask God to help you never to compare yourself to others.
- Confess the mistakes you have made as you have tried to run your race. Ask for forgiveness and humility to forget the past and press into the future.
- Invite the Holy Spirit of God to help you embrace your struggles and see them as part of the race—not a detour from the race.
- Lift up praise to God for victories you have experienced and for the progress you have made.
- Ask God to help you choose your life, delight in it, and not long for anyone else's life.

FINAL PERSONAL STUDY

Reflect on the content you've covered during this final week in *She's Still There* by engaging in any or all of the following activities. The time you invest will be well spent, so let God use it to draw you closer to him. Be sure to share with your group leader or group members in the upcoming weeks any key points or insights that stood out to you.

Celebrate Good Times

You will find that your race becomes more joyful and that you have more strength to run it when you choose to celebrate the good things along the way. Each step in the right direction is worth cheering! Every act of faithfully following Jesus is a little victory. So give yourself a pat on the back for your progress and commit to cheering others on in their race.

A Pat on My Back

There is nothing wrong with celebrating your progress, milestones in your growth, and positive steps forward. As a matter of fact, this is a good personal discipline. Take time today to write down five areas where you can see yourself taking strides and steps forward.

AREA OF MY LIFE AND RACE	STEP I HAVE TAKEN FORWARD
1.	
2.	
3.	
4.	
5.	

Once you have made your list, read through it slowly. Thank God for giving you power for each step of your journey. Celebrate the fact that you have been faithful and have continued your race. Then ask God to help you keep pressing on for His glory and for your good.

A Pat on Their Back

It is also good to celebrate the steps forward that others have taken on their journey. Think of one of your small group members who you've seen taking positive steps on her journey. How do you see her moving forward and becoming the girl God wants her to be?

Commit to encourage, bless, and give that person a pat on the back (it could be a note, a text, a call, a lunch out, or some other form of communication). Do this in the next week, and let God use you to lift up this sister and cheer her on as she runs her unique and God-given race.

Celebration is more than recognition. Celebration is the way you mark the moments of your life. It involves heartfelt experiences that create lasting memories. Those memories are the building blocks for your perception of your existence on this earth. You might be good at acknowledging a remarkable person or event in a culminating moment, but you are also a remarkable person, and your life is an ongoing remarkable event worthy of being celebrated along the way.

—*She's Still There*, page 260

From Comparison to Gratitude

All too often we compare ourselves to others instead of being grateful for what God has given to us and what He is doing in us. Make a list of three ways you are tempted to compare yourself to others. (Examples include physical appearance, possessions, gifting and abilities, education, spiritual maturity, friends, social standing . . . and so on.) Be honest, humble, and specific as you do this. Use the space provided to journal your confessions, and then look deeper to see what you have in that very area of life for which you can be grateful to God.

- **Area #1:** _____

Why I am tempted to compare myself to others in this area:

What I have in this area that is a gift, a blessing, and something to be grateful for:

My prayer to God thanking Him for what He has given me in this area:

- **Area #2:** _____

Why I am tempted to compare myself to others in this area:

What I have in this area that is a gift, a blessing, and something to be grateful for:

My prayer to God thanking Him for what He has given me in this area:

- **Area #3:** _____

Why I am tempted to compare myself to others in this area:

What I have in this area that is a gift, a blessing, and something to be grateful for:

My prayer to God thanking Him for what He has given me in this area:

When you and I compare ourselves with others, we engage in an activity that doesn't do anything to help us get where we want to go. We waste energy and emotions on something that takes away from us instead of building us up. When we engage in comparing ourselves with others, we're fighting a battle we're bound to lose.

—*She's Still There*, page 270

Leaving the Darkness, Walking in the Light

Each of us at times is tempted to cover up our sin. This is as old as the opening chapters of Genesis, when Adam and Eve tried to cover their rebellion and Cain tried to cover his murderous actions. The only way to return to running your race and choosing your life is to confess your sins to God and hold nothing back.

King David experienced this firsthand. Read 2 Samuel 11:1–12:13. After David had taken another man's wife, had her husband murdered, and tried to cover up his sin, God sent a prophet to confront him. At that moment, David could have kept running away and covering up his sin, but he chose to take a different course. He confessed his sin and turned his heart back to God. Shortly after, he penned the words of Psalm 51.

Reflect on this psalm as you read it slowly. Underline or highlight when you see the depth of David's confession, repentance, and brokenness.

> Have mercy on me, O God,
>   according to your unfailing love;
> according to your great compassion
>   blot out my transgressions.
> Wash away all my iniquity
>   and cleanse me from my sin.

For I know my transgressions,
     and my sin is always before me.
Against you, you only, have I sinned
     and done what is evil in your sight;
so you are right in your verdict
     and justified when you judge.
Surely I was sinful at birth,
     sinful from the time my mother conceived me.
Yet you desired faithfulness even in the womb;
     you taught me wisdom in that secret place.

Cleanse me with hyssop, and I will be clean;
     wash me, and I will be whiter than snow.
Let me hear joy and gladness;
     let the bones you have crushed rejoice.
Hide your face from my sins
     and blot out all my iniquity.

Create in me a pure heart, O God,
     and renew a steadfast spirit within me.
Do not cast me from your presence
     or take your Holy Spirit from me.
Restore to me the joy of your salvation
     and grant me a willing spirit, to sustain me.

Then I will teach transgressors your ways,
     so that sinners will turn back to you.
Deliver me from the guilt of bloodshed, O God,
     you who are God my Savior,
     and my tongue will sing of your righteousness.
Open my lips, Lord,
     and my mouth will declare your praise.

You do not delight in sacrifice, or I would bring it;
you do not take pleasure in burnt offerings.
My sacrifice, O God, is a broken spirit;
a broken and contrite heart
you, God, will not despise.

May it please you to prosper Zion,
to build up the walls of Jerusalem.
Then you will delight in the sacrifices of the righteous,
in burnt offerings offered whole;
then bulls will be offered on your altar.

What lessons do you learn from David's story?

In light of these lessons, take time in silent prayer to lift up your own confession. Keep Psalm 51 in front of you and let David's example help guide your prayer of confession.

To continue moving forward, you have to make up your mind to live in the light, to be honest with yourself about your tears, and then be vulnerable and authentic with others. Once you realize that something in your life has taken you off the path of decision, direction, discernment, and discipline and thrown you into a ditch, don't settle for staying there. . . . Find a safe place, and take off the mask. Reject the disguise, and be willing to be known.

—*She's Still There*, page 279

Recommended Reading

As you reflect on what God is teaching you through this session, review chapters 26–30 in *She's Still There*. Use the space provided to write any key points that stand out to you or questions that you wish to discuss with your group leader or another group member in the future.

ADDITIONAL RESOURCES
FOR GROUP LEADERS

Thank you for your willingness to lead a group through *She's Still There*! What you have chosen to do is important, and much good fruit can come from studies like this. The rewards of being a leader are different from those of participating, and we hope that as you lead you will find your own walk with Jesus deepened by this experience.

She's Still There is a six-session study built around video content and small-group interaction. As the group leader, imagine yourself as the host of a dinner party. Your job is to take care of your guests by managing all the behind-the-scenes details so that as your guests arrive, they can focus on one another and on interaction around the topic.

As the group leader, your role is not to answer all the questions or reteach the content—the video, book, and study guide will do most of that work. Your job is to guide the experience and cultivate your small group into a kind of teaching community. This will make it a place for members to process, question, and reflect—not receive more instruction.

There are several elements in this leader's guide that will help you as you structure your study and reflection time, so follow along and take advantage of each one.

Before You Begin

Before your first meeting, make sure the group members have a copy of this study guide so they can follow along and have their answers written out ahead of time. Alternately, you can hand out the study guides at your first meeting and give the group members some time to look over the material and ask any preliminary questions. During your first meeting, be sure to send a sheet around the room and have the members write down their name, phone number, and email address so you can keep in touch with them during the week.

Generally, the ideal size for a group is eight to ten people, which ensures everyone will have enough time to participate in discussions. If you have more people, you might want to break up the main group into smaller subgroups. Encourage those who show up at the first meeting to commit to attending the duration of the study, as this will help the group members get to know one another, create stability for the group, and help you know how to prepare each week.

Each of the sessions begins with an opening reflection. The two questions that follow in the "Talk About It" section serve as an icebreaker to get the group members thinking about the topic at hand. Some people may want to tell a long story in response to one of these questions, but the goal is to keep the answers brief. Ideally, you want everyone in the group to get a chance to answer, so try to keep the responses to a minute or less. If you have talkative group members, say up front that everyone needs to limit their answer to one minute.

Give the group members a chance to answer, but tell them to feel free to pass if they wish. With the rest of the study, it's generally not a good idea to have everyone answer every question—a free-flowing discussion is more desirable. But with the opening icebreaker questions, you can go around the circle. Encourage shy people to share, but don't force them.

Before your first meeting, let the group members know that each session contains three between-sessions activities that they can complete during the week. While these are optional exercises, they will help the members cement the concepts presented during the group study time and encourage them to spend time each day in God's Word. Also invite them to bring any questions and insights they uncovered while reading to your next meeting, especially if they had a breakthrough moment or didn't understand something.

Weekly Preparation

As the leader, there are a few things you should do to prepare for each meeting:

- *Read through the session.* This will help you to become familiar with the content and know how to structure the discussion times.
- *Decide which questions you definitely want to discuss.* Based on the length of group discussion, you may not be able to get through all of the Bible study and group discussion questions, so choose four to five questions that you definitely want to cover.
- *Be familiar with the questions you want to discuss.* When the group meets you'll be watching the clock, so you want to make sure you are familiar with the questions you have selected. In this way, you'll ensure you have the material more deeply in your mind than your group members.
- *Pray for your group.* Pray for your group members throughout the week and ask God to lead them as they study His Word.
- *Bring extra supplies to your meeting.* The members should bring their own pens for writing notes, but it's a good idea to have extras available for those who forget. You may also want to bring paper and additional Bibles.

Note that in many cases there will be no one "right" answer to the question. Answers will vary, especially when the group members are being asked to share their personal experiences.

Structuring the Discussion Time

You will need to determine with your group how long you want to meet each week so you can plan your time accordingly. Generally, most groups like to meet for either sixty minutes or ninety minutes, so you could use one of the following schedules:

SECTION	60 MINUTES	90 MINUTES
Welcome (members arrive and get settled)	5 minutes	10 minutes
Icebreaker (discuss one of the two opening questions for the session)	10 minutes	15 minutes
Video (watch the teaching material together and take notes)	15 minutes	15 minutes
Discussion (discuss the Bible study questions you selected ahead of time)	25 minutes	40 minutes
Prayer/Closing (pray together as a group and dismiss)	5 minutes	10 minutes

As the group leader, it is up to you to keep track of the time and keep things moving along according to your schedule. You might want to set a timer for each segment so both you and the group members know when your time is up. (There are some good phone apps for timers that play a gentle chime or other pleasant sound instead of a disruptive noise.)

Don't be concerned if the group members are quiet or slow to share. People are often quiet when they are pulling together their ideas, and this might be a new experience for them. Just ask a question and let it hang in the air until someone shares. You can then say, "Thank you. What about others? What came to you when you watched that portion of the video?"

Group Dynamics

Leading a group through *She's Still There* will prove to be highly rewarding both to you and your group members. However, this doesn't mean you will not encounter any challenges along the way! Discussions can get off track. Group members may not be sensitive to the needs and ideas of others. Some might worry they will be expected to talk about matters that make them feel awkward. Others may express comments that result in disagreements. To help ease this strain on you and the group, consider the following ground rules:

- When someone raises a question or comment that is off the main topic, suggest you deal with it another time, or, if you feel led to go in that direction, let the group know you will be spending some time discussing it.
- If someone asks a question you don't know how to answer, admit it and move on. At your discretion, feel free to invite group members to comment on questions that call for personal experience.
- If you find one or two people are dominating the discussion time, direct a few questions to others in the group. Outside the main group time, ask the more dominating members to help you draw out the quieter ones. Work to make them a part of the solution instead of the problem.
- When a disagreement occurs, encourage the group members to process the matter in love. Encourage those on opposite sides to restate what they heard the other side say about the matter, and then invite each side to evaluate if that perception is accurate. Lead the group in examining other Scriptures related to the topic and look for common ground.

When any of these issues arise, encourage your group members to follow these words from the Bible: "Love one another" (John 13:34), "If it is possible, as far as it depends on you, live at peace with everyone" (Romans 12:18), and "Be quick to listen, slow to speak and slow to become angry" (James 1:19). This will make your group time more rewarding and beneficial for everyone who attends.

Thank you again for your willingness to lead your group. May God reward your efforts and dedication and make your time together in *She's Still There* fruitful for His kingdom.

She's Still There

Rescuing the Girl in You

Chrystal Evans Hurst

What's a woman to do if her life is not taking shape the way that she thought that it would? What happens when she looks at herself in the mirror, lingering just a little longer than usual and realizes that she no longer recognizes the person staring back at her? What does she do when she sees that, somehow, her life has drifted away from all her original hopes, dreams, or plans?

Speaker, blogger, and writer Chrystal Evans Hurst wrote this book because she was that woman. One day she realized that she had somehow wandered away from the life that she had purposed to live a long time ago.

Chrystal since discovered that this moment of awareness happens to lots of women at different seasons of their lives. Poor decisions, a lack of intentionality or planning, or a long-term denial of deep hopes and dreams can leave a woman, old or young, reeling from the realization that she is lost, disappointed, or simply numb.

And she just needs encouragement.

This woman simply needs someone to hold her hand, to cheer her on, and to believe with her that she is capable of still being the person she intended to be or discovering the girl she never knew was there in the first place.

Chrystal uses her poignant story of an early and unexpected pregnancy, as well as other raw and vulnerable moments in her life, to let readers know she understands what it's like to try to find your way after some missteps or decisions you didn't plan on. In *She's Still There*, Chrystal emphasizes the importance of the personal process and the beauty of that path as it is shared authentically from one girlfriend to another. It's a book of "me too's," reminders of the hoped for, and challenges for the path ahead—to find direction, purpose, and true satisfaction.

Available in stores and online!